# NEWS FROM WHERE I LIVE

*Arkansas Poetry Award Series*

# News from Where I Live

POEMS BY
## Martin Lammon

The University of Arkansas Press
Fayetteville   1998

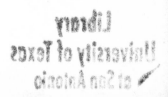

LIBRARY OF CONGRESS CATALOGING-IN-PUBLICATION DATA

Lammon, Martin, 1958–
   News from where I live : poems / by Martin Lammon.
     p.   cm.
  ISBN 1-55728-507-1 (cloth : alk. paper). —
  ISBN 1-55728-508-X (pbk. : alk. paper)
   I. Title
PS3562.A46434N48   1998
811'.54—dc21                    97-39769
                       CIP

*For my mother, for stories she tells me*
*For my father, for stories he keeps to himself*

## ACKNOWLEDGMENTS

I would like to thank the following journals in which poems or original versions of poems were first published:

|  |  |
|---|---|
| *Chariton Review* | "Naming Day" |
|  | "The Secret of Saturday Morning" |
| *Gettysburg Review* | "The Emperor's Dog Finds the Way Home" |
|  | "How I Learned to Count" |
|  | "Love in Slow Motion" |
|  | "What We Feel in Our Bones" |
| *Midwest Quarterly* | "Valley Falls" |
| *Mississippi Valley Review* | "When They Are Not Alone" |
| *New Virginia Review* | "A Japanese Woman Confides in Me and Speaks of Heaven" |
| *Nimrod* | "The Men of Springtime" |
|  | "Three Poems for One Traveler" |
|  | "Nearing Sixty, a Man Declares Himself a Romantic" Selected by W. S. Merwin for a 1997 *Nimrod*/Hardman Pablo Neruda Prize in Poetry. |
| *Ploughshares* | "Stories a Man Keeps to Himself" |
| *Raystown Review* | "In the Church of Saint Stephen" |
| *Southern Poetry Review* | "Where the Children Go" |
| *West Branch* | "Like New Gods, Two Japanese Women Guide My Hands" |
|  | *"Three Short Clay Poems"*: |
|  | "The Anagama Kiln" |
|  | "A Clay Bowl" |
|  | "What We Have in Common" |

I also wish to acknowledge the West Virginia Commission on the Arts for a 1994 fellowship in poetry that provided support during the completion of this work.

# CONTENTS

III. *The Way Back*

*I promised to show you a map you say but this is a mural*
*then yes let it be     these are small distinctions*
*where do we see it from is the question*
                    —Adrienne Rich, *"An Atlas of the Difficult World"*


           *Chia-Shun laughs also,*
*and closes the book, and says,*
*"When I see these pictures, when I remember these things"*
*—he looks like a boy, wild and pink with excitement—*
*"I want to live two hundred years!"*
                    —Donald Hall, *"Photographs of China"*

# I. *Crazy for Paradise*

# NEWS FROM WHERE I LIVE

*After reading Associated Press reports, Good Friday, 1991*

In Cutad, north of Manilla, six men
are nailed to crosses in a rice field.
A crucified fish vendor weeps
because his mother was sick
then well again.
                In the Colosseum, the Pope
carries a five-foot cross. Beneath
the Roman moon he leads a torchlight
procession, the long walk of Jesus to Calvary.

And in Jerusalem, Christians follow
the *Via Dolorosa*. Each carries a cross.
John Moore of Maryland walks beside
fifteen Arabian priests in black robes.
"You feel you have to whisper," he says.

~~~~~~~

Where I live the *Altoona Mirror* publishes
two photographs on the front page:

In the first, Tanya Glass, age nine, poses
like a tent revival evangelist,
and in her small hands the *Holy Bible*
opens like black wings; in the other photo
the girl spreads her arms as if she will fly
off the page. She is showing the way
Jesus (Jason McCauley, age seven) should suspend himself
on the cross he props on his back. What he carries
is a long forked stick, the kind a prospector
might cut for a rod to divine where water hides.

~~~~~~~

In Altoona, boys and girls practice for posterity
at birthday parties and the Bavarian Club Octoberfest.
Proud mothers and fathers preserve snapshots
in worn shoe boxes salvaged from Christmas.

Years from now, an old woman will shuffle
photographs stacked high as a pinochle deck,
let her finger pause on a girl's blurred face—
                    heal herself a little.

# IN THE CHURCH OF SAINT STEPHEN

You just never know what people will say. In Ebensburg,
Pennsylvania, in the Laurel Lounge, a woman tells me
she is lucky, how her father
never laid a hand on her; how in Cambria County
a girl is thankful if her father ignores her.

So we dance all Saturday night, hold on
to each other, and let ourselves go
to hell, and go happily
out into the dark parking lot. She says she can't
go home with a married man, couldn't live with herself
Sunday morning.

                    In the Church of Saint Stephen,
pews cut from Laurel Highland pine will not warp.
Joints and iron buckles will last, might as well
say so, forever. Old coal men who built this church
let their women shave them, their jaws and chins, gentle
as women can. Mines had turned skin raw. The sons of men
who built this church liquor each other up
with schnapps while their wives scheme ways to keep them
from coming home drunk and eager to work out their women
in bed, or hard against the kitchen floor.

In the Church of Saint Stephen, a father's palm clamps
around the pew's curved seat, his hand
so close to his daughter's
she thinks he might take hold,

a man I imagine on the steps of Saint Stephen,
finally articulate:

>    If I never took money from my kids' hands
>    for liquor nor tobacco,

*if I never took skin off their bodies*
*when I slapped my belt against them naked,*   ·
*if I never took my daughter down*
*into the cellar weeping,*
*I got more right to heaven than you*
*that never put up a church, nor bloodied*
*socks frozen to your feet in winter.*

Sober or drunk, I'd hold my own father if I could
to one promise. I'd lean down close, my ear
to his lips. He'd whisper, and then I'd sit down
beside his bed, wait for him
to die, his hand rigid
in mine, the good death I want for him. For me.

At the Church of Saint Stephen, I could sit beside
that woman I knew, hold her hand,
repeat for her my father's last three words,

a common phrase we'd hold him to.

## STORIES A MOTHER COULD TELL

The stories I could tell you, how your father proposed
that quiet night in April, 1956, warmest planting
anyone remembered. Your father drove
me home that night, swerved off the road
where tractors flattened a path
between cornfields. That spring, the land
plowed over, the soil was so black
farmers in Fulton County swore
come summer even fence posts might sprout.

Your father and I parked, quiet a long time—listened
to crickets, the radio. My bare legs itched. He told me to open
the glove box, and I found the ring he'd hidden there.
It was my eighteenth birthday.

How I wanted
out of my father's house, how I loved your father
that night, his kisses so deep I was dizzy, his hand
on my knee, on my thigh.

How in a '48 Ford I wanted all of him.

Now I live in a town I'd never
heard of when I was a girl. Not much anymore
dazzles a woman my age. I sing in the church
choir, and teach children
whose fathers played little league baseball with you, whose mothers
whispered about boys they'd marry—maybe even giggled
your name. Lord, that was twenty-five years ago.

But in that world I used to live in,
a mother held her weeping son, hugged
his heaving shoulders because she knew how,
soon, he would not let her touch him this way.

The stories I might tell you
I could not speak out loud. How one night your father
wanted all of me, how I knew
what he wanted, and what to do.

When you lie down with a woman, curtains closed, your face
so near she feels you breathing, I know what she feels
is the story a woman keeps to herself.

## LOVE IN SLOW MOTION

Today we are watching a movie. Mrs. Daniels
teaches us. Behind our backs her voice
fills the room the way God must sound
inside a priest's head. "You see,
children," she tells us, "it grows too slowly
for the naked eye, this miracle
science shows us." Here is what we see: a jittery
seed, its skin unpeeling, root and stem
wedging through dirt; leaves and petals
unfurling and blooming. I wonder
if the girl beside me notices the way I watch
her, how I want to kiss her cheek, how I worry
she will know what I am thinking.

~~~~~~

In the dark room, we lean
our elbows against carved wooden
desks, wobbly and stained. Others
have chiseled their initials here. The girl who sits
beside me, the one
I'd pass notes to if she loved me, yawns
and picks up her pencil. She digs the point into deep
grooves and daydreams about a boy who would love her
enough to leave letters dug into soft wood.

~~~~~~

In my science book there is a note card
pasted inside the back
cover. All our names are listed here, all of us
this book has belonged to. In 1958, the year I was born,
a girl took the book to bed. She would have worn
nail polish and lipstick. She would have read how

the food chain and photosynthesis
converge, how every animal metabolizes oxygen,
how the engines of leaves churn
sunlight and carbon dioxide into what we breathe.

How everything is invisible, incremental, and patient.

## WHAT A BOY MIGHT HAVE WRITTEN
## BEFORE HIS SUICIDE

When my hand follows the curve of her hip
I know how our teacher's formula fails,
how only the body explains
what's beautiful in this world. My bass guitar
thumps inside my chest, so deep I think fingers
pluck between my ribs. First period choir
is God's voice, soprano, alto, baritone, and tenor
the filaments that weave our chorus
together. When her mouth closes over mine,
I know what I know.

My love,
my fingertips burn where I touch your thigh.
When you lie beside me under stars, each needlepoint
of light pricks my bare arms. I remember once
a priest explained how a boy's eyes would go blind
if he stared into the face of God, and how I should not
be so curious. Once, my mother warned me
to look away from the sun's eclipse, said my eyes would
sizzle like bacon frying, only I wouldn't know
until too late. How can I face you

my love? Sometimes if I lie down
in the basement, if I close my eyes
in that dark place, I can almost feel nothing
but cold cement damp against my skin.

I am on fire
all the time. Whether this is hell or heaven
I cannot live here. I cannot breathe
this air. I cannot go barefooted. I cannot hold

my hands over my ears forever. This world is not
safe. But you are
so deep inside me that I am not afraid
I might only be crazy.

Is there a prayer for me? Keep it
for another—whisper those holy words
into his ear. I'll be there. I promise.
He will understand if I listen.

# SIGN LANGUAGE

The woman he loves holds his hand.
With her fingers
she spells "water," "mother,"
"I love you," and he learns
how Annie Sullivan
taught Helen the body's words
for the cool river
in July, for the soft shoulder
where daughter lay her head.

The woman he loves holds
his hand. She leans
her head down to kiss
each knuckle, the curve
between thumb and forefinger.

After a long rain cleans the air
and the night sky is open and cold, the shiver
along his neck when he looks up
and loses himself looking at stars
is the body's sentence: *I want to believe.*

Or, the muscular heart's:
*I am afraid*
*I want you more than this body*
*can withstand the pressure*
*of its blood.*

# WHEN THEY ARE NOT ALONE

Yes, right now
he wants to love her
in his worn
doctor's chair, where
long nights alone
he hunches
and types.

Tonight, they are
not alone
and he would
love her, right now,
just where she is
sitting, typing
her late report due
so early next
morning.

How he wants
to leave his body
out of this
work they must do

but the chair
swivels
full circle
on its oiled screw
and tilts
just far enough
instinct
seizes them. They

fall back
into the heart's
pulse, the shudder

they cannot resist when
their bodies are falling
into that deep
well of gravity
and longing.

# STORIES A MAN KEEPS TO HIMSELF

*. . . for it seemed to me that everybody ought
to know about it, but I was afraid to tell, because
I knew that nobody would believe me . . . .*

—FROM *Black Elk Speaks*

It's a strange night here in West Virginia, warm
for November, one last thunderstorm before winter
comes on. Rain rattles against metal
awning, as if Oglala drummers surrounded
my house. They pound hollow bones against skinned
logs. Perhaps long thigh-bones of Wasichu
killed last summer, or buffalo slaughtered long ago
after a boy's first hunt.

This is the way I think these days.
When I read what Black Elk dreams, and what he remembers,
I know something creeps into me that keeps me awake at night
and that I take with me when I sleep. How a Sioux man
falls in love with a woman and follows her even though
she will not talk to him. He hides in the bush near
the river where she bathes or washes clothes. He waits
for hours just so he can be alone with her and talk about love.
He offers a dozen ponies he does not have, or a hundred,
because he knows he will borrow or steal them if he has to,
just so he can love her forever.

I know I have no right
to that man's life, and that Black Elk did not live
or die so that I might make this poem. I am Wasichu, I live
in a box. My music is not his music, I have no fire, and I
could not kill a man even if I hated him. I'd be the first
to die in a fight, or hunting buffalo for three days in deep snow.

But there are stories I can't get rid of, so many lives
crowded inside me, not in my head
so much, but in my chest, where the Greeks found
the soul—*pneuma* they called it; "pneumonia" what we call
the sickness that steals our breath—and it is a kind of sickness
that Black Elk felt when he lay in fever for twelve days
and journeyed with his grandfathers, and that I feel
in the wing-bones of my hips the day after
I make love to a woman I'd give
anything to have beside me now. A hundred
nimble ponies.

But tonight there's just this strange rain
beating on my roof. The only other sound is moths
hurling their bodies against the porch light, as if lost
spirits possessed them, crazy for paradise.

# THE SECRET OF SATURDAY MORNING

It is a simple recipe, she says,
so I peek into her bowl
and, yes, even I can see
there is butter, flour, a little sugar,
and raisins. Do you like them?
she asks, and I know she means
the raisins, so I say
yes, but what I mean is

how beautiful you are
on a Saturday morning,
stirring a spoon slowly;
how it is the way your hand
turns and rolls, devoted to this
simple task, baking muffins
with raisins for us, and how
sweet I know they will taste,

but what I say is, yes,
and again, a little softer, yes.

# VALLEY FALLS

All morning, rain soaks the small river.
Water gushes over mossy rocks. For a moment
you think you might dance across
barefoot and fearless.

Old branches snap from trees and are swept away.
Old roots tangle in the bank's loose soil. You think
you might dig your fingers into this mud, hold
hands with a love you've waited for
since before you were born. The river

rumbles toward the falls. Blood
hurtles through the valves of your heart

and you think you could find a new life
inside the source of all falling water.

# THE MEN OF SPRINGTIME

*Ilira is the fear that accompanies awe;* kappia *is fear
in the face of unpredictable violence. Watching a polar
bear*—ilira. *Having to cross thin sea ice*—kappia.

—BARRY LOPEZ, *Arctic Dreams*

One hundred seventy years ago, European whalers
hunted *Balaena mysticetus*
in Pond's Bay, north of Baffin Island. The Greenland
right whale, or Bowhead, was slow; it floated
when killed; pound for pound, its bone and oil
made men rich. It was *the*
whale, the *right* whale, to hunt, but not easy
to kill. Whalers slaughtered thousands. The native
*Tununirmiut* called these strangers
"the men of springtime." By the summer of 1832
all the local villages were silent. The Eskimo
had died during the winter from diptheria and smallpox.

*Yaks* the whalers called them.

~~~~~~

Summer in West Virginia, the year I turn
thirty-five, my fears are common:

that I have lived for nothing more
than a small house I do not own;
that I shall die before I've written a poem
my whole life depends on;
that a woman I love will not speak to me.

Last March, when a blizzard
heaped snow against my windowsill, when I was
alone, when the evening air
was phosphorescent, I could not sit still.

All I could do was pace, shake, weep. I listened
to the white wind. A wave of snow
banked across my road, as if an arctic ocean
would swell over my house, swallow me whole.

~~~~~~

The men of springtime were seized by glaciers cracking, falling
like mountains into the sea; by white belukha whales
haunting like ghosts the keels of their ships; by *water
burning like manganese in the evening sun*. Many whalers
died. The Eskimo had lived
a thousand years in this place, had learned
words for *the fear that accompanies awe,
fear in the face of unpredictable violence*.

*Ilira. Kappia.* I look for words that will name
the fears my body knows, what only my body
can translate faithfully: How an unexpected
blizzard seizes me, or a woman's blue eyes—
the apparition of her face adrift in falling snow.

# WHAT WE FEEL IN OUR BONES

One night a woman tells me, "I wouldn't have the courage
to kill myself, or the instinct." Her fingers
stroke the bones that wrap around her eyes.
She rubs the hollows between bones.

I remember Senior Anatomy, the cat's
skeleton, how Mr. Mitchell traced his finger along
lumbar and thoracic vertebrae up to where the medulla
oblongata would attach to the neck's stem. The skull
looked to me like a girl's fist, and I wanted
to hold it in my hands, my thumbs laid against
each zygomatic arch—as if cheekbones might be
a portal to a new kind of heaven where
infinitesimal gods plotted inside a cat's head.

Where do you scribble an answer like that on the teacher's
quiz? What do you say to a woman
who rubs her eyes as if she'd stared too long at the sun,
or down, where new snow glitters
like god-fire? You say nothing. This is the way
love ends, the way your hands go numb,
then toes, the way an old man
feels in his bones there's no one
who will rouse him from his bed.

## II. *The Way to the New World*

# THE SECRET OF THE PLATYPUS

*What could this curious mélange be,*
*beyond a divine test of faith and patience?*
—STEPHEN JAY GOULD, *"To Be a Platypus"*

Outside my window, a hill
rises, the same
as every morning this summer.
I sit in my chair and read Gould's argument
for the marvelous platypus, whose species
dull biologists have relegated
to a lesser rank within *Mammalia*,
or I write a new poem
about mothers or fathers, cows
or trout. I lift up my head to look at the hill,
how it slopes above our neighborhood's
houses. I do not know how high
but steeper and wilder, I think, than I
could climb. I watch the dawn
fog dissolve into the haze of August.

The platypus swims across the river, lays
eggs in the mud, and does not love my poem.
The hill does not need me
wedging my boot against some tender
root. The shrub has its own life. One leaf
strains for a little sunlight. So what if I cannot
witness the way leaves work? I know they stretch and curl
for one day's glory all their own, even if I don't
know how. And if I did sink my boot into mud
where no one had ever walked before, no photographer
or archeologist would celebrate that I had
climbed this hill. The maple, if it noticed me at all,

would shrug and endure my hug around its trunk, a man's
simple panic against gravity.

This morning, I sit in my chair
and read about the platypus, whose strange wet fur
glistens in the moonlight, or I write a poem about a beautiful
woman. There are so many lives whose secrets
do not belong to me, lives beside my own
whose secrets are worth loving.

# A JAPANESE WOMAN CONFIDES IN ME AND
# SPEAKS OF HEAVEN

Two hours by car outside Tokyo, where wind
ripples through rice fields, where silhouettes of cows
float across the ridge at dusk, Grandfather's house
is rubble now. In the backyard there was once a wooden shed
he hammered together before the war when he was just twenty-two.
Inside the shed, he'd bathe in a giant iron pot.

As a girl, I'd listen to crickets when,
half behind the horizon, the sun turned the sky red.
The breeze was cool against my skin. Inside the house
I'd tuck myself under Grandmother's arm and beg for a bath.
She'd smile and walk out to the backyard for firewood.
In half an hour she'd return, the water ready, and I'd see her face
smudged where she wiped her cheek hot from the fire.

I'd walk outside barefoot on the damp grass
to Grandfather's wooden shed, whose boards were swollen
and split by summer heat and winter snows.
I'd tug open the door and there it was, huge and black.
The iron pot, rusted here and there,
looked like a giant injured beetle crouching
above a fire's embers. All alone,
I'd undress, fold my clothes over a chair,
then rinse my body with cool water in the sink.

If you bathe in an iron pot, you must squat
on a wooden plank wedged into the curved bottom
or the metal will burn you; if you never soaked
in a giant iron pot, or watched the autumn stars
through crevices in a thatched roof, you cannot know
why I sang so loudly. A lady of the neighborhood cried,

"Stop singing such a clumsy song!" I am embarrassed
to tell you, I broke wind in the hot water, bubbles gurgling up to my chin.

They are dead now, Grandfather and Grandmother, but I tell you
Heaven is a giant iron pot
where old men and women soak and sing
and are young again. There's water enough
that I could join them. I am not afraid of dying.
Heaven is curved, and deep enough to bathe in.

# LIKE NEW GODS, TWO JAPANESE WOMEN
# GUIDE MY HANDS

Their fingers flutter
like feathers, like a boy's prayers.
Crane's wings lift and wave.

They hand me paper,
square wafer I twist and crease—
where is calm water

for the crane I make?
I pucker and blow on wings,
a Japanese wind

inhabits me here,
what claim have I on the air?
New gods are welcome

in my house and sit
at the head of my table.
Let us feast and share

our oldest stories:
a paper crane soars at night—
why not? Two women

guide my hands, we love
the creatures our fingers shape.
The old prayers, we keep:

"Very beautiful,"
they say, and *Hai,* I say yes—
human holy words.

# FROM WEST VIRGINIA, A FURTHER
# WESTWARD JOURNEY

A woman tells me
how sometimes she feels so small
on a starry night.

We walk together,
laugh—now and then I turn
my head, and she smiles

the way I love. She
is shivering. The night is cold.
I want to tell her:

*I will make a fire*
*for us from driftwood we find,*
*then lie down beside you*

*on the sand, look up*
*and say nothing, just listen*
*to Pacific waves.*

She tells me again
how the stars are hard to see
in Japan—that place

where she used to live,
so far away now, so close.
She says, "I want to

"show you Kyoto,"
and I want her to teach me
the secrets she knows,

shrines that are sacred
to millions of wanderers,
how to eat noodles

and rice, how to give
your shoulder to a stranger
on a crowded bus.

When I hold her close
to me, her body opens
a world that is not

small, but hard to find.
The fire burns low. Shadows.
"I want to see you,"

she says, after we
make love. In the dark, we lay
new wood on the fire.

# Three Poems for One Traveler

*tabibito to*
*wa ga na yobaren*
*hatsushigure*
                    —BASHŌ

I .

Blue Hole Cave, my guide tells me,
is for beginners. He points to a wedge
between rocks, tells me this is the cave's
mouth—and I believe him. You cannot
walk upright
through the opening. You lie back, slide
your legs through, scoot
down a small, dark gullet. My guide
explains how caves breathe, the science
of pressure and temperature,
of equilibrium. I do not tell him
how I hear a strange
sigh, as if a man were in
love or had just finished
a good supper of rice
and fish. I decide for myself
the cave's name is
a man's, and that I can
almost pronounce his name.

2.

There are no vowels in ancient
Egyptian writing—those sounds
were made by breath, sacred
in that old tongue. So when we write
in English letters *hekau*
we diminish
ourselves. We cannot imagine
a language of braided rope, hands
lifted up in praise, a bound
scroll, or remember how these hieroglyphs
inspire our translation: *Words of power*.
We are dispossessed
of the heart's muscle, of hands
that could stretch up to heaven, of hoarse
windpipe. We say *spiritus*, or how the hieroglyphs
inspire us, but we are not afraid enough
of God's breath, the *hex*
that animates our lungs
when love seizes us.

*Traveler,* Bashō asks
to be called, *when winter's first showers*
*change to snow.* There is so much
I have to learn, so much
my body knows.
My teachers help me
laugh again
and tremble
the way a man in love
laughs and sighs
in the same breath. How did this happen,
that I am in love for the first time
with a woman, and not
the idea of a woman?

One long breath
is enough for me
to recite the old *hokku* for all of us
travelers: *fallen leaves,*
*we do not know*
*when the wind will take us.*

# Cafe Negro at Soda Pininini

## THE MAN WINSTON McCLOUD, HE KNOW

### The Way Lizard Breathes

Lizard's tail twitches, tests the air.
Lizard's tongue tastes gnat's nearness.
Lizard's ribs squeeze in and out,
rapid as hummingbird's wings.

### Magical Realism in Cahuita, Costa Rica

"Jesus Lizard," they say here.
*Basilicus* run
fast. He skim over water.

### Realism Solo

"Lizards, what do you call them?"
I ask. Winston McCloud
say, "We call dem lizards."

# WATER COCONUT KNOW WHAT COMING

*Pipa*'s branch look like bird's wing—
palm leaf, like many feathers.
When air ruffle, just two leaves
twitter. The rest are still.
"Rogue breezes," crazy gringa tell me.

# ONE LANGUAGE

In Spanish, say: *ma-CHE-te*.
Again: mah-CHAY-tay.

Machete open pipa,
or swipe yard's long grass.

Machete make wide arc
like sun in the sky.

No *chistes* today. No jokes.

# THIS IS THE WAY HE SPEAK

Morning, man with machete
cut tall grass. All day
he sweep blade side to side.

This is the way he work. Man
with long stick knock down
oranges. This is the way

he eat and drink when sun is
high and hot. His bike
lean beside mossy pipa.

When sun go down, man pedal
slow on muddy road.
This is the way he get home.

# ALL THE NAMES I DO NOT KNOW

*Flora, Fauna, Frog*

Bananas ripening here,
green going to yellow—
how *rana* learned its name.

*Dendrobatid*

Long name
for thumb-sized, shiny
rana. Almost missed you
hidden among leaves
close to muddy path.

Maybe Talamanca coast
*Cabécar* men, or
*KéköLdi* tip arrows
with rana's poison.
I don't know. Many old ways

are lost here, same as back home.
But dendrobatid
is not lost. Its small body
knows how shocking green
can be, like no Ohio frog.

# THE FIRST THREE NAMES OF RAIN

Are not my father's spitter, his name for when
the lake's bluegill love best to nibble; nor clever holler
preacher's gullybuster, coal miner's altar call; nor even
come bedtime, your sweet grandmother's angel's tears.

Morning, my love and I learn how rain lures us
back to bed, how rainfall's rhythm beats
against palm branch, metal roof, banana's
leafy elephant ears. We sink beneath a gravity of rain.

Afternoon, rain soaks grass and wood, leaf
and juice maker. Rain muddies the slim path
in the forest, swells *gambas*, those spiral roots that twist
like fingers out of damp soil, merge, become the *Chonta* tree.

At night, before rain reaches your house,
you hear ocean and storm roar together, those two great waters,
and wait for rain to sweep over beach and tall *cocos*. Today,
or *mañana*, just wait: Maybe you learn the first three names of rain.

# Three Short Clay Poems

## THE ANAGAMA KILN

There is a difference. In America
most clay bakes in gas or electric
brick kilns, fires faithful
to knobs and valves. The Japanese Anagama

is a wood-burner, looks like a bunker
a crazy man built against angry gods,
or a giant mud dauber's nest. Every hour
day and night, men and women trade shifts,
stoke the kiln, pile on split logs,
scrap wood. The watchers peer inside,
gauge heat, and learn how fickle
fire is. In the Anagama a hundred pots,
plates, cups, and shapes—fish head,
turtle shell, dragon coil—blister and crack
or harden like fossils wedged in old mud.

At night, anxious potters whisper in the dark
glow of fire they are faithful to.

# A CLAY BOWL

In Japan, a Master's hands
sink into wet clay which spins
out into a bowl on the potter's wheel,
thumbs hollowing out the place
where rice will steam, or flowers
gather into one new fragrance
then wilt and spoil
as flowers must do. In Japan

a Master's clay bowl, fired and glazed
in the Anagama kiln, is beautiful
enough to serve supper in, to hold
what withers under the sun.

## WHAT WE HAVE IN COMMON

In the house I grew up in, my mother
surprises us when she mixes
her good Wedgwood dishes—a wedding gift
twenty summers old—with the cracked
plates stacked recklessly in her cupboard.

My mother tells me how, on her father's farm,
she shimmied on her knees in the baked Ohio dirt
and snipped green beans from the vine
for ten cents a row, and how
she dreamed of china patterns, delicate
coffee cups she would pose
behind glass panes of a cherry oak
cabinet. Older now, she gives in

to common sense, in America
the place where wealth
and poverty may be forged
in fiery fables we learn to spin
in the flickering rhythm of summer's heat
as if pedaling the treadle of the potter's wheel.

# III. *The Way Back*

# NAMING DAY

Each of us holds on to what we have
lost, our first language, the one
we were born with, loose
and rattling somewhere inside us.

Years ago, my grandfather's supper prayer
was a mumble, only his *Amen*
sounded safe. We drank *millich*
from Sterling's Dairy—*scheiss,* he'd mutter
if his daughter sassed him.

All these years
I did not understand my mother's
first name: *Licht-en-wald,*
a clearing in the woods.

One night I dreamed
I was speaking German.
I opened my eyes
and I knew
I'd understood every word.

Grandfather hadn't been dead long. And me?
I turned out the lights, went back
to sleep. That morning, I woke up
to crying, the old smell of milk.

Children toddle, swoop, and holler
in the yard next to mine. I cannot
guess what they are playing, their games
no more familiar
than the first time I balanced a bicycle, or the first
time I made love, and nerves fluttered.
One girl wanders away from her friends, stares
as if she sees
the woman she will become.

A willow tree or mulberry bush revives the old farm
where my great-grandfather
sits in the rocker on his porch, watches
the tiny cousins play tag among
shrubs and weeping willows.
He leans forward and calls:

*kommenkinder, kommenkinder.*

He is enormous, red-faced. A bald scalp
slopes down his forehead. Spotted and hairy
hands reach out to me. The cuffs
of his sleeves recede halfway to his elbows.

When I was three years old, my mother wanted me
to look this man in the eyes. They were
the color of roots dug out of loose soil.

Somewhere in a country I do not know, near
the Volga River, they tell me
there's a cemetery this man's mother is buried in,

where a stone cross marks her grave. And somewhere
nearby, her mother is buried, and another, and another
woman's mother—someone my life depends on.

There is no book that can prove this,
just stories women tell you.

# HOW I LEARNED TO COUNT

In the Ohio I know, the one nobody jokes about, Ralph Keefer
farms five hundred acres and holds on to that land
the way he grips a wrench. His right wrist,
cracked twenty years ago, has locked in place, so stiff
his arm and shoulder jerk and twist, half his body
devoted to the one small chore, tightening nut and bolt.

If there's a joke to tell here, it's on me, a college boy who
        once figured
he'd round up Keefer's heifer. One morning, sunny and dewy,
there she was like a statue in my yard, grazing on the tall grass.
Who could blame her? Not yet a year old, only half as high
as a man at her shoulder, white and black hide slipped tight
        around her
joints and slender neck, she simply longed after that unmown,
foot-high feast untrampled and so green it must have seemed
        heaven to a cow.

How she finagled her way through barbed wire
there's no telling, but that morning, I looked out my window
and knew what to do. I eased the door open to sneak
up and corral her. Forty feet between us, she swung her head
        toward me,
looked me over, the bristles on her chin moist, her jaw
grinding. Drooling at the corners of her mouth, she chewed
on what to make of me, no doubt, her wide eyes the size of walnuts.

I don't know how to talk to a cow. I know now there's no
pleading "Hey bossy, there, there, bossy," sidling closer, holding
out an empty hand. Even a tender-hoofed cow knows what
        you're up to.
And me? What I thought I'd do if I caught her I couldn't tell you.

Crook my arm around her neck? Haul her back to the fence,
       hold apart
the barbed wires while she sank to her knees, shimmied back
       to her pasture?

Lucky for me she kept her distance. So when I panicked,
figured I'd charge her, all there was to live down
was confessing to Keefer how I'd run off his heifer, last I saw
her back legs kicking up gravel and dirt a half-mile down our
       county road.

You go visit the Ohio I know. In Athens County, farmers swap
       this tale
about a cow that outsmarted a college man who couldn't figure
       simple arithmetic.
Ralph Keefer will tell you, if you dare hope hold on
to what you have, you must learn to count:
One man can tighten just one bolt at a time.
One acre yields two hundred bushel of corn or nothing.
One potent bull satisfies twelve heifers.
Most every time, four legs outrun two.

# NEARING SIXTY, A MAN DECLARES HIMSELF
# A ROMANTIC

He wishes his wife would rise
from her patio chair, walk
next to him, sit on his lap. She might
whisper how the full moon
shines so beautifully, how
it is the color of his hair.

He wishes their son would visit
his garden. He would show him
this year's rows of green
beans, sweet corn, and
carrots—"Miracles,"
he would say.

He wishes their daughter would listen
to his stories and hear how
he tries to make his voice
slow and lonesome, like Benny
Goodman's sweet clarinet.

Does anyone know how he grieves
for the moon, or the way dirt
feels between his fingers? Does anyone
know the story he is writing
in his head, the hero
he would have been
when he was a boy?

Nearing sixty, he still loves
to fish the deep lakes near the house
where he was born. He wakes up
at dawn and does not return

until dark. Today, he climbs into
his small boat, dips oars
into the lake, and rows
the way his father taught him,
soundlessly, pulling
slowly against the weight of the water.

He wishes his father could see how his large
hands make perfect moons
in the air around him, how everything
circles back, how his whole body
rocks in heroic rhythm to his rowing.

I squat where the grass grows
thick and soft, beside the pond
where trout swim near the horizon of air
and water, eyes like onyx pebbles,
mosquito or waterbug reflected there.

Ganglia tingle in the trout's brainstem—

*what bolts down*
*spine, ribs, fins; the swift flip*
*of jawbone—*

          which is the splash
that turns my head, that shocks me
before I know why, the glimpse
of tailfin, ripples in the water
where my father taught me to aim
my cast. This moment
I hunt
for whatever horizon there is
between history and my heart.

# LOOKING FOR THE LANGUAGE OF WATER, WALKING, OF LOVE

Where I grew up in Ohio, my grandparents would have called this
    water I walk beside
a crick—a word my father also used for the ache in his back after
    he'd watered
and hoed his garden from sunrise to noon, his two boys dawdling
behind him, not worth a lick—also a word for where animals
    gather, so I've heard
about this place, Kelly Creek, where a twelve-point buck's craving
    might be settled.
I am in South Carolina, out State Route 56, where I think a man
    might beg
for a licking if he looked the wrong way at another man's wife
    or sister.
It was like that in Ohio, too.

In better English, you could say *stream*. You could say *spasm*. You could
describe piquant boys worthless to their father laboring in his garden.

You could say *brawl*.

I walk down Kelly Creek, keeping close to the water. I follow the
    path
I'm given, sometimes over slippery rocks, over sandbars, sometimes
    farther
from the bank, picking my way around trees, bamboo stalks, kudzu,
and briars—*prickers* I called them when I was a boy.
I love this walk today in South Carolina, a far piece from Ohio, or
    the walk last month
in the Blue Ridge Mountains with the woman I love, or in West
    Virginia
where I live now, where I dally as often as I can near the river
    and hills

at Valley Falls. This kind of walking, you keep your eyes to the
    ground—someone else
might think you were ashamed—but you just never know what will
    seize you, a kind of moss
you've never seen before, or gopher hole that would snap your
    ankle. You have to love
each step. You look for the rock that won't come loose, the root
    that will hold,
dirt that will pack down under your boot and won't slip where you
    dig in.
Nose to the ground, you pause. You stoop, squint down the seam of
    a raw pod
about to bust open, plump seeds so red you want to find a new
    name for that color,
*not* scarlet, *not* magenta, but something else, no word yet for what
    you've pinched between your fingers.

Should I have said *burst*?

There is a language people made for this place, for walking, and for
    love, an art
I'd like to hold onto, making words for what I find when I walk, for
    what keeps me
coming back to these creeks and gullies and hollers.

*Spider's Lace. Knuckle stalks. Backbone stones.*
Not gurgle, not babble, but how the water has a tongue that licks
inside my ear when I stand still, listen. *Feather moss.* The nervous bird
with no name, wings that waggle inside my chest
when I see the woman I love, like walking on water.

# NO DOMINION

Across the East Coast of America, the honeybee—*Apis
mellifera*—has died. Mites have infested the hives:
the *varroa*, big enough to see, wedges in the creases
of a bee's body; the *tracheal mite*, microscopic
but more deadly, lodges in the throat, chokes.

Beekeepers' hives are empty. The fields
are quiet. No ecstatic buzz among dandelions
or black raspberries. In the white dutch clover
bees do not dance for each other, mapping the journey
to pollen and nectar. Keepers visit their silent
apiaries, nostalgic for living shelves of bees
they held between their gloved hands
like old priests at their altars.

On an island in the Chesapeake Bay, scientists breed
new queens from Yugoslavia, three hundred dollars
for one imported bee. They are packaged
and safe in tiny boxes, one bee each. Scientists experiment
with hybrids, resilient but gentle, their honey sweet.

Last week, a woman tells me, she found
among the deep-blue stars of borage
flowers, dancing among the leaves that taste
like cucumbers, honeybees, a small cloud
hovering and buzzing there. She does not know
where they come from—a wild hive, she guesses—bees
luckier, or stronger, than their engineered cousins,
a hive of *Apis mellifera* whose instinct and desire
are older than Roman words
for bee, honey, for what is born wild.

# THE EMPEROR'S DOG FINDS THE WAY HOME

In my neighbor's yard, a pug dog sniffs
clipped grass. Its whole body swivels
in a circle, as if an axle plumbed
from the dog's center of gravity
straight through bedrock, magma,
down to the molten core.

And why not all the way to China?
Lingering in this breed is the scent
of the Emperor's hand massaging wrinkled skin
on the pug's neck, the Forbidden City's aromas—
silk, spice, incense, the familiar
odor of god idling on his gold throne.

Now the dog lies down, the whiff of mown grass
deep in its snout. The pug rolls and digs
its shoulder into the ground for the joy
of scratching that thick hide, its body
unfolding like West Virginia's hilly horizon.

# AN EQUATION FOR HOFSTADTER

*Now you may feel a little dizzy—but the best is yet to come.*

—DOUGLAS HOFSTADTER,
*Gödel, Escher, Bach:*
*An Eternal Golden Braid*

On Backbone Mountain, the ridge
I drive across each day, I slow down
mornings winding
my way to work. The car
tilts into the curve's
ascent against mountainside.

Loggers' trucks grind gears. Pavement
blisters. At the berm, asphalt
crumbles and flakes, mixes
with gravel and cinder. The guardrail
is a cable as thick as my forefinger
strung between wooden posts
two feet high. You might be saved
if the cable twisted around
a wheel or bumper.

                    The mountain road
is like the sand-track a desert snake makes:
a wave
of sine and cosine coiled
on a meridian. The fractal
path up the mountain
is like a dystrophied spine.

Slow down. I promise
the mountain gives ground enough.

# NOTES

"In the Church of Saint Stephen": See Acts 7:51: "As your fathers did, so do you."

"Stories a Man Keeps to Himself": The word *wasichu* is used as a racial slur, a usage glossed over in *Black Elk Speaks*. John G. Neihardt provides only this note: "A term used to designate the white man, but having no reference to the color of his skin." I use the word to mean "other" or "stranger," but I must also accept the slur: "I have no right / to that man's life . . . I am Wasichu . . . ."

"The Men of Springtime": When I take essential terms or phrases from Barry Lopez's *Arctic Dreams*, I try to acknowledge with italics or quotation marks where these do not interfere with the poem. I am indebted to Lopez for his marvelous book.

"A Japanese Woman Confides in Me and Speaks of Heaven" is for Masumi, a former student of mine at Fairmont State College in West Virginia, who wrote the lovely essay from which this poem steals much of its language and all of the story.

The sequence "Three Short Clay Poems" is for Jack Troy, who once admonished me to write a short poem for a change. "A Clay Bowl" was the result, to which Jack responded, "I like it but I think it needs to be longer." Hence, *three* short clay poems.

*Three Poems for One Traveler* is for my wife, Libby Davis.

*Cafe Negro at Soda Pininini* is dedicated to Lloyd Wright Daley and his wife, Rosa, who owned the *Soda* (lunch counter) near Cahuita, Costa Rica, where one could find a good cup of black coffee, hear (in English and Spanish) Lloyd's lively stories and Rosa's good advice, use the public phone to call family and friends anywhere in the world, and flag down the bus to San José. Thanks also to Winston McCloud, who knows about a lot more than lizards.

"Naming Day" and "Where the Children Go" are *in memoriam,* Wilhelm ("Bill") Lichtenwald, my mother's father. The Lichtenwald family is descended from the Volga Germans who retained their native culture and language after they emigrated to Russia's Volga River Valley.

"How I Learned to Count" is for Ralph Keefer, a storyteller and leg puller.

"No Dominion": Thanks to Valerie Nieman and John King, bee charmers both.